How to Become a Ticket Broker

By Mike Omar

This ebook was brought to you by http://makemoneyfromhomelionsclub.com.

If you are interested in entrepreneurship, making passive income online, and other ways to make money outside of a standard job, be sure to visit http://makemoneyfromhomelionsclub.com!

In the first video lesson you are taught the entire process of how http://mikeomarphotography.com was made from beginning to end, without the need of any coding knowledge, in under one hour!

With the lessons taught there, you will be able to make yourself a professional website with any kind of look that you want.

There are also lessons on Search Engine Optimization (SEO), social media promotion, making mailing lists, selling ebooks and other digital products, developing passive income online, and more. There are also lessons on how to make money with Google, Amazon, and ClickBank (all passive!).

My books:

HOW TO MAKE A WEBSITE OR BLOG: with WordPress WITHOUT Coding, on your own domain, all in under 2 hours.
http://makemoneyfromhomelionsclub.com/ebook1

HOW TO MAKE MONEY ONLINE: Learn how to make money from home with my step-by-step plan to build a $5000 per month passive income website portfolio (based on building 10 websites that make at least $500 per month each).
http://makemoneyfromhomelionsclub.com/ebook

HOW TO START A BLOG THAT PEOPLE WILL READ: How to create a website, write about a topic you love, develop a loyal readership, and make six figures doing it.
http://makemoneyfromhomelionsclub.com/ebookblog

Table of Contents

Introduction.....6
Research.....7
    Questions to Consider.....7
    What are some of the best places to research?.....9
Legal Matters.....12
    Legal Issues Selling Tickets.....12
How to Buy Tickets like the Pros.....13
    Ticketmaster.....13
        Ticketmaster Online.....13
        Ticketmaster Outlet.....15
        Ticketmaster Phone.....16
    Presale Tickets.....16
    Sporting Events.....17
How to Sell Tickets like the Pros.....20
    When should you list your tickets for sale?.....20
    How to List Your Tickets on Ebay.....21
    Other Ebay Tips.....26
    Other places to sell your tickets.....28
    Make a Website or Blog.....28
    How to Buy a Domain(s) and Hosting.....30
    Installing WordPress.....34
Conclusion.....40

Introduction

Thank you for purchasing my e-book! Here you will learn a lot of valuable information that has taken years of experience to accumulate, and then quite a long time to write out as well! Just like everything in life though, the beginning will be the hardest part. The first couple of months are the hardest, but keep trying, don't give up, and you will find that it becomes easier and easier. With time, you can become a ticket broker for a living and your own boss as well.

This book has been written based on my own personal experiences and of other ticket brokers that I know. It contains everything I know about the business, and it would have helped me immensely if I had this when I first started! Be sure to read the book carefully and take the information to heart; there are a lot of details that are easy to miss the first time through. Also, refer back to this book regularly as you go through the entire process over and over so that you develop good habits.

Good luck on your journey to running your own business and being your own boss!

Research

Research is arguably the most important part of this whole business, and it is why most people can never become successful as ticket brokers; they don't do the research! There are many things you want to be paying attention to when considering the purchase of tickets to an event. When you first start, it may be a little overwhelming to be thinking about all these things, but it is important to point them out now and keep them in mind, even if it is hard for you to make judgment calls this early in your ticket brokering career. Eventually with tracking and experience, you will learn to start thinking about all these questions.

Questions to Consider

1. What are the other events at that city that week? Is there another major event going on the same weekend as the event you're considering reselling? Maybe that same night? Which one is bigger? If there is another event that same night in the same city, that could negatively affect your sales, and you may want to let both events go.

2. What is the size of the venue? Will this event sell out or will there be seats available in the nosebleeds the day of the concert? How do the best seats and worst seats of the venue compare in price or value? Are they similar or are the best seats clearly worth more money?

Depending on the event, some venues you will want to buy any tickets you can get, others only if the seats are good, and others you will pass on (very hard to do when you get your hands on good seats, but it is a habit you must develop!).

Sometimes a small venue can be great news for you if it is a decent sized event. Maybe an up and coming band with a loyal fan base couldn't book the big venue – that's great news! In that case, getting some good seats could make you more money than if you had gotten good seats at the bigger venue.

3. What kind of market are you dealing with? An area with money? A saturated area? How has that event done at that venue in years past? You will have to start tracking these things so you can refer to your own data year after year.

4. What kind of a following does the event have? Some events have die-hard fans that won't miss a show and will pay big money for good seats. Other events people will buy as something fun to do, but are more indifferent. Events with those types of spectators have buyers that will NOT pay big money for tickets. Be careful spending a lot of money on events like those, you could end up losing BIG time.

5. What day of the week is the event? This makes a big difference! A Friday night event will have much higher demand than a Tuesday one - even with the same exact artists!

6. How often do these events occur? U2 only tours every five years or so. The world cup is every four years. The Superbowl is only once per year. Those are all no brainers - you always buy those tickets! Make sure to do your research! If a group just toured through a city four months earlier, then tickets probably won't sell for nearly as much.

Some events are no brainers like the superbowl, U2, or Shakira - if you can get good tickets to those events, you will profit. The questions above are for middle-sized events (regular season sports tickets, Matchbox 20, Linkin Park, things like that). You need to be able to ask yourself those kinds of questions for those middle sized events and decide whether those tickets are worth buying.

When you get good at identifying which tickets are good to purchase at the middle sized events level, that is when you will start to make some good money! This is because most events are middle sized - anyone could have made a profit off of the Michael

Jackson concert that was going to happen right before he died (RIP MJ). That was a no brainer, but most events are not. This is why tracking is so important.

If you want to do this for a living, you need to start studying trends and tracking your results. I know the above part may seem like a lot to think about, but make sure to start considering these things and thinking about them! Analyzing these questions over time will make you a better ticket broker in the long run, so pay attention to those details!

I WOULD HIGHLY RECOMMEND WRITING EACH ONE OF THOSE SIX QUESTIONS DOWN ON A SHEET OF PAPER AND THINKING ABOUT EACH ONE BEFORE PICKING OUT THE EVENTS YOU ARE GOING TO GO AFTER.

Believe it or not, thinking about each of those questions critically every time you consider an event is what will eventually make you a GREAT ticket broker (unlike so many ticket brokers out there that are throwing darts in the dark). Eventually it will be second nature for you, and you will be able to judge events quickly and effortlessly, but at first it is important for you to think about each question one by one and start honing your skills.

What are some of the best places to research?

Your own tracking files of past events! Yes, to do well in this business, you need to start tracking your own sales.

For those of you that may not understand what I mean by tracking, it's very simple. Keep a record (on Excel or something similar) of the tickets you've bought and sold. Keep track of the event, face value, sale amount, venue, seat sections, date, and day of the week (each of those criteria is a column).

At first you may not know how to judge and value these things, but after a while you will start to have a pool of data, and also start to understand it and learn how to read it. This will make you great at judging which events to buy tickets for in the future. You'll soon realize some venues always do better than others, or always worse at certain times of year, things like that.

Obviously you don't have any records at first, which is a reason this business can be difficult to start off in, but that's ok. After you've been tracking yourself consistently for a while, you'll definitely have a real feel for how this business runs and works. This is partially because you'll have your own records to look back on, but also because this habit forces you to think and analyze your purchases.

TRACKING IS A VERY IMPORTANT HABIT TO DEVELOP; DO NOT SKIP IT. IT WILL FORCE YOU TO ANALYZE YOUR WINS AND LOSSES AND MAKE YOU A BETTER TICKET BROKER.

At first, you're going lose some money on tickets, but that's when you learn the most - when you fail. So don't be afraid to try some things, but also (and I can't stress this enough):

When you start, only work one event at a time! It can be VERY tempting to buy two tickets for one event, four for another event, two for another event, etc., without any sales yet, and before you know it you're $1200 in the hole and it just became critical that you sell those tickets. TRUST ME - waiting to see if those tickets sell can be very frustrating, especially if you are counting on a return. As a beginner, I would recommend you never have more than $400 worth of unsold tickets (so two events, two tickets each AT THE MOST).

Obviously once you have done this for a while, you'll be comfortable with much more money invested at once.

Besides your own tracking, here are some other websites you will want to do some research at:

Pollstar.com - This website is a great place to start reading, and I go pretty much every day (it's my newspaper). I would highly recommend you start getting to know that site very well and visiting daily. It talks about the biggest tours of the year, when new tours are announced, biggest sales of the week, year, etc.

Ticketnews.com - Very similar as poolstar; this is another site I would start visiting daily.

Those two are really the only two I would recommend. They're the best and other websites will say the same things those do. There is a lot of overlap between what those two websites say, but between the two of them, you'll be in the loop about what is going on in the events world.

EXTREMELY IMPORTANT TIP:

Before you go to purchase tickets for an event (once you have done all your research), decide beforehand what are the acceptable seats to purchase for that event.

If you decided only the first 10 rows will make you a secure profit, stick with your plan! If you go to purchase tickets and find two tickets in row 14, I know it can be tempting to purchase those tickets, but stick with your original plan! This habit can be hard to develop, but it will give you a much more secure business overall. Learn to walk away from a sale empty handed, follow your own guidelines, and don't sway!

Legal Matters

Legal Issues Selling Tickets

Ebay strictly follows the rules of each state, which means you are subject to those rules as a ticket broker if you want to use Ebay (you do!).

It is absolutely legal to sell tickets for up to their original ticket price anywhere in the US.

It is legal to sell tickets for more than their original price in MOST states, but not all.

You will have to look up your state law to check that you are not in one of the unlucky places that doesn't allow it.

However, if you are, don't worry! While I am not endorsing this, I have heard of others doing the following to get around that rule:

Open your business in another state and buy a P.O. Box in that state. Since this business is not one that requires a storefront, you can basically operate from anywhere. Problem solved!

I would also recommend reading up on Ebay's official standing on this here:

http://pages.Ebay.com/buyselltickets/faq.html

And finally, last but not least, you DO NOT need a license to resell tickets.

Sell your books at sellbackyourBook.com!

Go to sellbackyourBook.com and get an instant price quote. We even pay the shipping - see what your old books are worth today!

Inspected By:adela_qc

00069100851

How to Buy Tickets like the Pros

One of my favorite sections! How is it that the pros manage to get all the good tickets and the fans never can?

Well, the trick is actually very simple, and now that I'm on the other side of things, I can see perfectly well why ticket brokers do so much better than the fans. This is because most event ticket buyers only do it once or twice a year for the event they care about! You, as a ticket broker, will be trying to purchase the best seats for tickets to events almost daily! Of course, you will do a much better job than they can.

While they're fumbling around trying to figure out how to buy a ticket, you will be sitting at your computer the SECOND the clock strikes 10 a.m. (or whenever your event goes on sale).

Ticketmaster

To put it bluntly, Ticketmaster controls this entire business (not literally, but may as well), so you just have to learn their system and play by their rules to get your hands on good tickets.

Ticketmaster Online

Before you try to purchase tickets for your first event, go to www.time.gov and sync your computer with the time on there (that is what Ticketmaster uses), and make sure you get the Atomic time on your computer synced up (make sure it shows the seconds).

Obviously, first you create an account on Ticketmaster (say yes to their newsletter option to get news about upcoming events, etc.).

Then go to www.broker20.com and download their Broker Browser (free). This will allow you to open as many windows as you want with different cookies in each one. This is important because Ticketmaster.com can tell if you are using different browsers based on the session cookies (but not if you use the Broker Browser!). This is a huge advantage over the regular ticket buying crowd, and even a lot of other ticket brokers.

Type in the web address for your Ticketmaster.com event and open it in 10 different windows (if you set the view to tile them horizontally, you can see them all at once).

Here is what you do: if the event ticket sale is set for 10 a.m., have all this ready by 9:59. I'd recommend getting on at 9:45 the first few times around until you get the hang of it.

The SECOND your clock hits 10 a.m., start looking for pairs of tickets in the "best available" section in each of your different browsers.

Don't hit refresh too often on the same window or Ticketmaster will block your IP address and lock you out of their system for a full 24 hours - not good. This is why we set up this whole thing; you can't do what we're doing with only one browser open.

Trust me, learn how to use the Broker Browser - this is a HUGE advantage to have over the rest of the population.

Once you start getting REALLY serious with this business (maybe after a month of experimenting or so), I would recommend using the Insomniac Browser for buying tickets online. It isn't free like the Broker Browser, but once you reach the point where you are purchasing more than two sets of tickets per week, it will be worth it to subscribe. The Insomniac Browser lets you pull tickets in through as many tabs as you want and you can rotate through tabs very quickly, allowing A LOT of submissions per event. Click here to check out what they have to offer and different pricing plans (I would recommend watching their video "are you getting 8 pulls per minute?" to get an idea of how powerful this tool can be). They have a free trial version so you can give it a shot before purchasing.

Ticketmaster Outlet

Nobody seems to believe me when I tell them, but going to the actual Ticketmaster outlet is one of the best ways to get tickets. Most cities have one, and if you want to check if yours does, just visit Ticketmaster.com. If you live far away from a major city, you can still be very successful at this business, but you don't get to take advantage of the Ticketmaster outlets.

If you find out there is one near you, you have to find out a few things (a quick phone call will tell you).

1. What are their hours of operation? This is to make sure you don't get out there at 9:50 a.m. on a Saturday only to find out they're closed.

2. What venues can they sell tickets for? Some outlets only sell tickets for venues in the city, sometimes it's for an entire region; you need to find out.

3. Is your event blocked for a short period of time? Sometimes an outlet won't sell tickets for another until after a half hour period has passed from the initial sell time. In this case you would have to go for to the computer or the phone for tickets.

Some extra tips:

1. Always call before to make sure they are selling your tickets at this time, etc. This will save you a lot of headaches!

2. If you show up before the ticket sale time, and the line is more than five people long, you may as well go home (or call while you are waiting if you don't want to give up).

3. Make friends with counter people! This can help you in huge ways once they start to get to know you! Trust me. ;)

4. Bring a venue map! This will help you out tremendously when they tell you what seats are available to you - you can make a much better judgment call at that moment.

5. Just because you drove there and waited for 20 minutes does not mean you must buy tickets! If the tickets aren't in the section you decided was worth it before you came, just walk away!

Ticketmaster Phone

To be perfectly honest, this has been my least successful way of purchasing tickets. You have to go through a ton of automated operators to finally get to a real person, and the timing has to be pretty lucky once you're put on hold. I would recommend calling half an hour before the sale time, and your best bet is if you get someone live, convince them to wait for you while the ticket sale time approaches. Overall though, I'd say stay away from this method and stick with the other two.

Presale Tickets

Getting presale tickets is extremely important if you want to be successful in this business. The good news is, this can be easier than getting tickets through the usual manner! Presales happen all the time, but as long as you are paying attention, you probably won't miss any of the major ones, and this is another way to stay ahead.

One of the easiest ways to get presale tickets is through the fan clubs. One thing that you will have to do is join the fan clubs of all the major artists online, but don't worry, most of them are free! When you first start, I would recommend just joining the free ones, and once you start getting more accustomed to becoming a ticket broker, go ahead and join the rest.

Once you are part of the fan club, you will generally be notified of presales for your group (a lot of times they will be sold on Ticketmaster a few days before the regular sale, and you will have to submit a password provided by the fan club). Some fan clubs don't allow you to resell the tickets you got through the presales, so with those, you'll have to sell at your own risk (although I've done it and never had any trouble).

Besides joining the fan clubs, here are other great sources for presales:

Venues - Go to major venue's websites and sign up for their venue mailing list. They will send you some great deals that you won't get anywhere else.

Livenation.com - Once you are a member, you can sign up to receive emails announcing presales for whatever artists you want (at first, just sign up for the biggest artists).

Credit Cards - These days almost all the major credit cards offer something special involving tickets for big events, but the major one I would recommend is American Express. Look into their programs to see what kind of offers they have, but being a Gold member has gotten me some really great tickets to major events (offered exclusively through their program). This one you'll really have to do a little research and figure out what you can get based on your credit history. But if you can get a good American Express card, I would highly recommend it.

Sporting Events

College Football Bowl Games

These tickets are actually purchased well before the teams are chosen (in the summer or fall), but this is actually not a bad thing. The reason? Almost all the games between Jan. 1 and Jan. 8 are good games with crazed college students dying to go. This is a pretty safe bet in terms of profits if you can put away some money for that long (remember, you're purchasing these tickets in the summer and not selling until late December or January).

All you have to do is look up when the tickets go on sale, and purchase them exactly as described earlier through Ticketmaster. The major ones are the ones that start Jan. 1 and those are the ones you want to buy (Capital One Bowl, Orange Bowl, Fiesta Bowl, etc.). The Sugar Bowl always seems to be my best earner so I'd definitely recommend that one.

If you manage to get BCS tickets, you are pretty much guaranteed a profit. Even the worst seats will get at least double your initial investment.

Bonus news about the bowl tickets: If you manage to get tickets to a bowl game, you can pretty much become a season ticket holder for that game! Why? Because you will be contacted by that bowl in the spring asking if you would like to renew your tickets, and sometimes even upgrade! That means you pretty much have a guaranteed profitable set of tickets each year after that.

NCAA Final Four and Regional

These tickets are also sold off-season and at face value. You just have to go to ncaasports.com and submit an application into their lottery. The only downside (aside from not being guaranteed a ticket) is you have to pay before you get the tickets. If you don't win, they just refund the money. You can apply up to ten times, but you have to pay each time. If your wallet goes that deep, I would certainly recommend it! These tickets are an easy return on your money as well.

Seasonal Tickets

Seasonal tickets can be VERY profitable, but also take a large investment to start off. I would certainly hold off on buying season tickets for any team or sport until I was a little more seasoned of a ticket broker.

That being said, you can make some very serious money with certain teams. Baseball, NBA, NFL, and college football can all be very good earners with the right teams. For baseball, the Red Sox and Cubs have the best return, followed by the Yankees. For NFL it would definitely be the Packers (however, they have a waiting list over 20 years long to get their tickets). College football it really depends on the season.

Really what you're hoping for is that your team goes to the playoffs - that's when you can make some really good money. Unless you can get season tickets for any of the teams mentioned above (which are sure ones), I would avoid buying season tickets unless you are very confident that team will make it to the playoffs, or you live in the area and are a fan anyway. That is really ideal, because then you can go to the games yourself if they don't sell (or if your team makes it the playoffs, and you decide this time you'd rather go than sell your ticket!). I've picked going to the event many times instead of making easy money - its one of the perks of this business, you do what you want!

The Superbowl

The granddaddy of all events for the professional ticket broker! If you can get tickets for the Superbowl, you WILL make money. The way to apply is to send a letter with your information on it to a P.O. Box sometime between Feb. 1 and June 1 of the year before the Superbowl you are trying to attend (i.e. - make this a yearly habit). The address has changed over the years a number of times, so the easiest way to find the address is to just type the query into Google. If you are lucky enough to get selected, you can buy tickets to the Superbowl at face value! Make sure your letter is sent by either certified or registered mail, and it includes your full name, address, phone number, and email.

How to Sell Tickets like the Pros

How and when you list your tickets online is one of the most important parts of the business. There isn't anything necessarily hard or complicated about it, but I definitely see a lot of other ticket brokers making very simple mistakes that are costing them A LOT of money. Its not that they are not bright, they just aren't thinking like a ticket BUYER.

When should you list your tickets for sale?

The answer is immediately after you purchase them! Why? Because this is the day a lot of fans tried to get tickets, and either couldn't get tickets because the concert sold out or could only get awful seats that they didn't want. They immediately jump onto Ebay when the demand for tickets is high; they're blood is still hot and they're in buying mode!

Now there are some people who will wait to put them up for sale until right before the concert, but this is bad for two reasons.

1. It's much more risky; there is a much higher chance you don't sell the tickets.

2. The die-hard fans who HAVE to go to the event and who will spend the most money have already purchased the tickets. You will be dealing with more casual ticket buyers at this point. So basically, as soon as you confirm those great tickets from waiting on Ticketmaster, you go straight to Ebay to list them!

One last reason not to wait: sometimes if the concert is an immediate sell out, they will announce a second concert in the same venue. This means you will almost certainly not make a profit on your tickets, and possibly not sell them at all. You want to have sold your tickets before a second concert is possibly announced.

Note: This does not apply to events that are wayyyy in advance (duh!). If you purchased college bowl tickets in the summer, obviously you want to wait a week or so before the event to sell them, once the teams are announced!

How to List Your Tickets on Ebay

Here I will show you EXACTLY how you need to list your tickets online in order to maximize your sales.

Love it or hate it, Ebay will be your main place to sell tickets online. Understanding and utilizing Ebay regularly is a good skill to have, and it is essential to this business as well.

Here is the step-by-step guide on how to create an Ebay listing for your tickets:

Title

Once you did some research and were able to get some great tickets, it is time to put them up for sale on Ebay. There are three things you want to put in your title every time: the name of the event or band, the word "tickets," and the city the event is in. Sounds simple right? You would be shocked how many listings forget one of these three things! And that means that a lot of people searching for their specific event aren't seeing that seller's listing.

Each title allows up to 55 characters in the title, and I suggest you use them all. Once you have those three initial things (title, "tickets," and city), the next thing you want to include is the venue name. If at this point you still have space, put down something about why your tickets are good (floor seats, five rows from stage, SEC 1, etc.). Use every single character you are allowed to squeeze in as much information as possible about those tickets.

Adding a subtitle is only $.50 and I highly recommend it. You get another 55 characters and I recommend you use them all. This will also make your listing stand out more.

Search for a Product

A pretty cool thing Ebay does is allows you to search for the product you are selling, and almost always there is a listing for your specific ticket event. Just select tickets, and then event tickets, and It'll have your event listed so you can select it and move on.

Add a Photo

Ebay will list a photo of the floor plan of the venue, and this will be just fine for our purposes, since your product description will include your seat details.

Describe the Item you are Selling

To start off, you want to make sure to include all the following in bullet points:

*Event title and performers (or teams, etc.)
*City and Venue.
*Date of Event.
*Seat Details.

Don't write a description; make it a list with bullet points. This will make you look more professional.

Include a payment policy. I personally only accept Paypal, and since most people use Paypal, it keeps thing simple. I also state that I expect payment within seven days of the end of the auction (a reasonable amount of time).

Include a shipping policy. If you choose to charge the buyer for the shipping, make sure to state it here! Also include the other details about your shipping policy here (I list my personal preferences below).

Include a return policy. The return policy I use is "We only accept returns for events that have been cancelled, and at the face value of the ticket. We will not accept returns due to rain-outs or postponements of the event. The tickets must be returned within seven days and the buyer is responsible for those shipping charges." This is much more comforting to a buyer than just not accepting returns at all, which could cost you a lot of sales. Plus if the event is cancelled, you will still have made the additional money from the buyer, and hopefully get the refund from Ticketmaster.

Also include some general information like this: "Positive feedback will be left immediately upon payment. If you have any questions, please email us before bidding."
Include an "about us." You can also include links to your other ticket auctions and ask them to make you a favorite seller.

Remember: to become a professional at this business, you need to treat this like a business. Start creating a brand and a following for yourself.

Once you have done this a few times, you will get to know your personal preferences for all these options (shipping policy, payment, etc.); I'm just writing what I recommend or go with personally.

The whole point of setting up the listing like this isn't just to lay out your rules and protect yourself (even though that's a part of it), its also to create CREDIBILITY as a serious seller; this will lead to more sales. A person who sees your product and another similar product will go for the more professional looking page, even if the professional looking page has the more expensive product.

Here is another good trick if you're having trouble: go to top sellers on Ebay and just emulate their templates to fit your product. All the major sellers have shipping policies, information about their company, etc., and they all have that professional sound you want in your listing as well.

Set a Price, Length of Auction, and Shipping Details

Everything before this was the easy stuff. This is where I see others with all kinds of varying strategies to sell their tickets, and making HUGE mistakes. Pricing and timing is really everything in this business; it can make or break the sale. What's the best option? List the tickets at right below face value in a bidding auction. This will almost guarantee at least one bid and usually leads to a good profit.

You know why this is a good strategy? I can pretty much guarantee the tickets sell, so I at least break even, but a lot of times the final sale of the tickets is much higher than my initial price. This is because when people go on and they see I already have bids on my item, this creates trust that I am a legit seller on Ebay. If they see my auction has 12 bids that has driven my price up to $300, and the listing next to mine is at $300 with no bids, they'll be drawn to my auction and bid for my tickets.

I see initial bidding prices all the time of twice the face value or more of the tickets with no bids at all, while my auction is increasing well higher than those auctions. We have the same product; they just listed it wrong. And not only is it costing them profits, it could even result in a loss if the tickets don't sell at all.

How long should the listing auction last?

The best length is three days. Here is why: as you already know, you are putting these up for sale the day the tickets went on sale (when the demand is highest). As I suggested earlier, you should only be purchasing great seats (good at the lowest quality). This means that when you list them on Ebay, your listing will offer some of the best tickets; you want to make sure your tickets are visible to everyone searching, and Ebay lists their auctions in terms of what listings are ending the soonest. Your other two options are 1 day and 5 days. 5 days is too long, and because your auction isn't expiring soon, it won't show up in the top results; something you don't want. 1 day isn't a bad option, and arguably better than 3 days because you'll show up higher in the listings, BUT I like 3 days because it gives fans a few days to decide if they'd rather spend more money on better seats, or just spend less money on the tickets still available on Ticketmaster. If they decide to go for the better seats, your auction is still up and rising in price!

The only time I would suggest going for a 1 day sale is if the concert immediately sells out and the demand is really high. Because those bidders want to make sure they get their tickets, they'll want to bid on tickets with a faster ending auction.

Buy it now?

This option is really up to you. It can't hurt to put this price at something you know you'd be happy with (like 3 times the face value), but just make sure not to cut yourself short if you have some spectacular tickets. Middle-center-front row tickets to a huge event could bring you money like you wouldn't believe! If you have tickets like that, DO NOT use the Buy it Now option.

Shipping

Always ship with tracking or a confirmation number, plain and simple. Without this, you have no proof you ever sent anything, and if a buyer complains, you will lose your money (Paypal will side with the buyer). Plus this gives the buyer peace of mind so they can track the item they purchased.

I give the buyer the option to choose how I will ship it, and I usually charge them the shipping. I highly doubt they will not make a purchase of several hundred dollars and then back out because of the shipping price.

Return Policy

Make sure to check the box that says "add a return policy." It would be easier to say we don't accept returns, but I think this might dissuade some purchasers from making to bid (the return policy we have is the one we wrote in the item description).

Also check the box that says you want to block bidders who might make the transaction more difficult or expensive. This will block people who have a bad history on Ebay - why risk it?

At this point, you will click continue. It will give you one last chance to review your information and give you the cost. Then just confirm the listing, and it will go live!

Other Ebay Tips

Credibility is the name of the game. If you have a professional looking landing page, you will most certainly increase your sales; a lot of people are still wary of buying things off of Ebay. Here are some other ways to increase your credibility:

1. Increase your feedback score. This one is a bit tricky, but we all had to start at zero. With every positive sale you make, the higher your score gets. One way to fast-track your way to a high score instead of plowing your way through is like this (or something similar):

Sell maps for a penny. My friend did it with free NYC subway maps. He'd pick up like 10 everyday on his way to work, sell them for a penny on Ebay, get a positive review, and just pay the postage stamp to send it. He had over 100 positive reviews in less than a month from people who were planning a trip to NYC and needed a map.

2. Include a logo in your listing such as the buysafe.com or squaretrade.com logos. Honestly, there are a bunch of logos like this that you can include for a fee, or if you abide by a certain policy. I would recommend adding a few to your listing - a lot of them don't even charge you unless you make a sale. The point of these is not so much about what they actually stand for; it's more about making your listing seem more credible.

3. Answer your emails in a timely and professional manner. A lot of times the question is already answered in your product listing, but the buyer just wants some peace of mind before he bids by talking to a person. Just be professional, answer his question, and he will more than likely bid if he likes the answer.

Sometimes you will receive emails saying you are a scalper or a bad person for denying true fans the chance to go. Just politely reply that you bought the tickets the same way anyone else could have and that your original bidding price was below the face value; there really isn't much more than can say. Don't potentially tarnish your own reputation by replying with anything nasty; they could forward that email to Ebay and you could get your account in trouble.

Now that you've read all this, you're probably thinking most of this stuff is pretty straight forward, and the truth is, it is! However, putting them all together is what will put you miles ahead of all of your competition. You already know when to list the tickets, for how long, and at what price to maximize your sale. You also know how to list it so that it will be viewed and found by the most buyers. Lastly, you have an extremely professional landing page that creates credibility in your integrity as a businessperson, and this will hopefully create a loyal following to you from consistent concertgoers. All this things coupled together make for a very powerful sales force on Ebay. If even one of these things is missing, it could jeopardize your entire sale, and what you will find in this business is a lot of other listings missing just a few of those crucial ingredients.

Other places to sell your tickets

Stubhub - To be perfectly honest, I go here AFTER the tickets didn't sell on Ebay. If they didn't sell on Ebay, I tend to list the tickets on here at face value because they really weren't winners (my judgment was poor in purchasing). That being said, Stubhub is also an easier place to list and sell tickets and it is pretty self-explanatory (not much strategizing here, all you do is list the ticket and price for a flat fee). However, as someone who is looking to make the most profit he can, I would certainly recommend you list your tickets on Ebay first, and look here only as a secondary option.

Craiglist - This is basically a last ditch effort if you couldn't sell on Ebay or Stubhub. This is truly a shot in the dark, but it is another option if you're desperate. If you're selling them on here, it's a pretty good chance you're going to sell at a loss.

Make a Website or Blog

If you really want to be a big time ticket broker, you need to make a website and blog for your business (both can be on the same URL).

In today's modern era, a website is absolutely crucial for marketing yourself. Launch a website that displays tickets you are currently selling, all linked to your ebay account. This will also create credibility for your business.

You should also make a blog for your business. You can quickly generate tons of traffic by providing useful information regarding upcoming events. Give visitors a reason to comment. Social networking sites and online newsletters can all advertise your services without bleeding your pockets.

If you can develop regular traffic or a following for your blog, this could give you considerable leverage in your industry and can be a catalyst that takes your career to the next level. Blogs have a habit of bringing unexpected opportunities!

Making a website or blog is actually a much simpler process than it used to be, and you can make yourself a professional one with any look that you want in less than a couple of hours, even if you aren't very good with computers (and you don't need any coding knowledge to do it!).

This is possible because of WordPress. For those of you that have never heard of WordPress, it is a content management system that makes it extremely easy to build and update websites on your own domain.

Note: When I say we will be creating a website using WordPress, I don't mean creating one through the WordPress website. Websites created through there are severely limited in what you can do with them and offer very little flexibility overall. The method I teach enables you to create truly professional websites by installing the WordPress software and you won't be limited in any way.

Let me put it this way: if you can use Microsoft Word, you can build and maintain a website or blog using WordPress! And there is no need of coding knowledge at all to do it!

Over 15% of all websites on the Internet were made and currently operate with WordPress!

To install WordPress on a domain you own doesn't take more than 15 minutes, and someone who knows what they are doing can make a professional website in less than one hour.

Note: The following chapter is the beginning of my other ebook "How to Make a Website or Blog with WordPress WITHOUT Coding, all in under 2 hours!" If you would like to purchase that ebook to get access to ALL the lessons on WordPress, you can purchase it here: http://www.amazon.com/Mike-Omar/e/B008CA6EPK/

Note: Everything you need to build a professional website or blog can be found on my YouTube video series at http://makemoneyfromhomelionsclub.com (lessons 1.1 – 1.4). I only mention the ebook for those of you who want extra WordPress training in ebook form.

Note: If you are interested in learning how to start a blog that develops a loyal following, you can purchase an ebook on that topic here: http://www.amazon.com/START-BLOG-THAT-PEOPLE-ebook/dp/B00BFNE0N4/

The following lesson on how buy a domain, buy a hosting account, connect the two accounts, and install WordPress can also be found in video form via YouTube on this page (lesson 1.1): http://makemoneyfromhomelionsclub.com/lesson-1-1-how-to-make-a-website-or-blog-without-coding-using-wordpress/

I suggest you watch that video in addition to the reading below.

How to Buy a Domain(s) and Hosting

The following lessons on how buy a domain, buy a hosting account, connect the two accounts, and install WordPress can also be found in video form on this page: http://makemoneyfromhomelionsclub.com/lesson-1-1-how-to-make-a-website-or-blog-without-coding-using-wordpress/

I suggest you watch that video in addition to the reading below.

There are two things you need to buy in order to own and operate a live website: the domain and the hosting. The domain of the website is the URL or the website address (i.e. http://www.example.com). A standard domain will cost you about $15 / year.

The hosting is where all the information and content of your website is stored. This information is stored on a server somewhere (a server is basically a giant computer) and you pay to rent out some of the space. A standard hosting package will cost you about $10 - $20 / month. Those are the bare essential costs associated with owning and operating a website.

A good place to buy both of these products is Black Steel Hosting. They offer any available domain names and high quality hosting at a good price and offer 24 / 7 tech support (which is really nice to have whenever things go wrong and you aren't a technical person, like me!).

To start the process of registering a domain and hosting, first click here: http://makemoneyfromhomelionsclub.com/blacksteelhosting

You can also find a link to their website under my resources page here:

http://makemoneyfromhomelionsclub.com/resources

Just go to "Domain Registration and Hosting" and you will see a link to Black Steel Hosting there.

After clicking on the link, you will redirected to the Black Steel Hosting homepage. In the center of the screen there will be a blank box where you can type in any domain you are looking for.

Note: Don't just read along without doing anything; actually build yourself a website now, even if it's just a practice one for fun!

Once you have typed in the domain you want, press the big green button "Search." If the name is available, at the next screen you will see it written in green; if it isn't, you will see it written in red. You can also get the same domain with other endings if you want (.net, .org, .biz, etc.).

Note: If you are interested in developing a brand for your domain, it might be a good idea to buy the .net and .org as well as the .com, even if you don't build anything on those domains (this is simply so nobody else can build a website there). You can just check off all the ones that you want and click on the drop down on the right to specify how long you would like to register each domain for. Once you are finished adding all the domains you want to your cart, press "Order now" to get to the next screen.

Note: If you are going to buy more domains, you'll have to get to the end of the checkout process to the "Order Summary" page, then press the "Continue Shopping" button instead of the "Checkout" button. There you can click on the "Register Domain" link to order more domains before checking out.

On the next screen "Domains Configuration", you have the option to add "ID Protection" to your domains. The way the Internet is set up, by default all websites publicly list the information of the owner (name, address, phone number, etc.). The only way to block this information from being publicly available is to add the "ID Protection." This will keep the owner's personal information anonymous and block people from being able to find it. Whether you get "ID Protection" for your websites or not is a personal preference, but I like to buy it for my websites.

The "Nameservers" below can be left as is and then press "Update Cart."

The next page is the checkout page, but we've only bought the domain(s) so far, so now we need to buy the hosting. Go ahead and click "Continue Shopping."

At the next screen you'll be taken directly to the "Web Hosting" link. Here you are going to pick between three levels of hosting (depending on your needs). The smallest package is for a single website, so if you know for a fact that you are building only one website, go for that one. The middle package can host up to 10 websites, and for most people reading this, that will be the appropriate package to get. If you are going to be building more than 10 websites, go for the largest package.

Once you select the hosting plan you want, click on "Order Now." On the next screen at "Product Configuration" click on the option "Use a domain already in my shopping cart" and then pick any of the domains you are buying from the drop down menu. The domain you pick will be the main one associated with your hosting account (although it doesn't matter which one you pick...just pick one). Then press "Click to Continue."

On the next screen you'll be at the "Product Configuration" page and can pick your billing cycle. The way the payment plans are set up, the longer you buy in advance, the cheaper the monthly price, so I'd go for at least a year.

Below that, you have the option of adding on the "Backup Restores Program" or "Professional Script Installation." The backups might be a good idea if you are not very tech savvy and would like to be able to have Black Steel Hosting back up your website to any previously saved backups (in case you mess something up). You also have the "Professional Script Installation" option available if you would like Black Steel Hosting to install WordPress on your domain(s) for you. If you opt for that option, you can skip the "Installing WordPress" chapter. :)

Once you are done, go ahead and press "Add to Cart" and continue on until you get to the final checkout page.

Before pressing "Checkout", some of you may need to get an SSL

Certificate. SSL Certificates are for people who need to protect sensitive information that customers will be submitting through your website. Examples include any kind of website where people are submitting personal or credit card information to buy a product, or any kind of website where people are entering login details (membership websites / forums), or any kind of e-commerce website. For any websites like that, you'll need an SSL Certificate (to protect your customer's information).

If you don't need an SSL Certificate for any of your websites, go ahead and press the "Checkout" button and complete your order. If you do need an SSL certificate for any of your websites, click on the "Continue Shopping" button and then click on the "SSL Certificates" link.

Here you will find different levels of SSL Certificates available and can read the descriptions to figure out which one most suits your needs. Once you have picked the one you need, press the "Order Now" button and select the domain you want it for. Then proceed to the checkout page.

At the checkout page you can review your order and make sure everything looks good. If you need additional domains or want to add anything, just click on the "Continue Shopping" button. If you are all set, click on the "Checkout" button and pay for your products.

Note: Write down the password you create during the checkout process, as you will need it soon!

Once you've finished checking out, you'll get to a confirmation page, and you're all set!

Installing WordPress

The next step is to install WordPress on your domain(s.). First go back to the Black Steel Hosting website and click on the "Client

Area" tab. Go ahead and login with your email address and the password you created during the checkout process.

From this area you'll be able to access the products you already own, buy more domains / addons, upgrade hosting, and open support tickets if you need technical support. This is your main "homebase" area where you will start to build your online business from. :)

Once you are logged in, go to the "My Products and Services" page (under "Services", then "My Services"). Your hosting account should be listed there, and then press the "View Details" button of your hosting account. Once you do that, click on the "Login to cPanel" button and a new page will open up.

Note: If your browser says "not safe, do not proceed" or something like that, just ignore it and continue to your cPanel.

Once you are at the cPanel, you're going to scroll down and click on the button that says "WordPress" under the "Softaculous Apps Installer" category. Then press "Install."

These are the options you should pick when installing WordPress:

Choose Protocol: http:// (or if you got SSL, then pick https://).

Choose Domain: Pick the domain you want to install WordPress on. At first, there will only be the domain that your hosting account is associated with. After installing this first one, I'll show you how to install WordPress on your other domains.

In Directory: Make it blank.

Database Name: Leave as is.

Table Prefix: Leave as is.

Site Name: Pick the name of your website (can be changed later).

Site Description: Pick a tagline for your website (can be changed later or left blank).

Enable Multisite (WPMU): Unchecked.

Admin Username: Pick something (but don't leave it as "admin"!).

Admin Password: Pick something (make it hard!) and write it down somewhere.

Admin Email: Your personal email is fine (can be changed later).

Select Language: This is your preference.

Limit Login Attempts: I would recommend checking this. This installs a plugin that helps prevent brute attacks of people trying to figure out your username and password by temporarily blocking people who have messed up the login information three times in a row.

Under the "Advanced Options" area (these can be chosen based on personal preference, but I wrote down my preferences below):

Disable Update Notifications: Unchecked.

Auto Upgrade: Checked.

Auto Upgrade WordPress Plugins: Unchecked.

Auto Upgrade WordPress Themes: Unchecked.

Automated Backups: Once a week.

Backup Rotation: 4

Then press the "Install" button.

WordPress should now be installed on your website! If you type in your domain into your web browser, you should see a plain looking website without any actual information on it except for your website title and a "Hello world!" announcement in the middle; that is the default WordPress installation.

If you are NOT seeing the default WordPress installation, there are a couple of things you can try first before contacting technical support:

1. Clear the cache on your browser and then reload your website. If you don't know how to do this, just search how in Google with whatever browser you're using (for example search for: how to clear cache on browser Google Chrome or how to clear cache on browser Internet Explorer). It should only take a few minutes to clear your cache. Once you do this, try reloading your website to see if you now have the default WordPress installation on there.

2. Wait some time. Sometimes it takes a while for the whole process to complete with the new domain connecting to the servers and then the installation process. It supposedly can take up to 24 hours for all of this to complete, but I've never seen it take longer than a couple of hours.

Note: To add WordPress to other domains within your account, you have to do one additional step. Within your cPanel, go to "Addon Domains" under the "Domains" category. Once inside, type your domain in the "New Domain Name" box (you must have already purchased this domain earlier and it must be within your Black Steel Hosting account).

In the "Subdomain or FTP Username" box, pick a username and write it down somewhere.

In the "Document Root" box, the information should have auto-filled in after you typed in your "New Domain Name", so just leave it as is. Then pick your password (make it hard!) and also write it down somewhere. Then press the "Add Domain" button and you are set.

Now start the exact same process as earlier, by scrolling down to the "WordPress" button under the "Softaculous Apps Installer" category. :)

Note: These past 4 chapters are the first 4 chapters of my other book "How to Make a Website or Blog with WordPress WITHOUT Coding, all in under 2 hours!" If you would like to purchase that book to get access to ALL the lessons, you can purchase it here:
http://makemoneyfromhomelionsclub.com/ebook1

All the remaining lessons on how to make a website can also be found at http://makemoneyfromhomelionsclub.com **in video form (lessons 1.2 - 1.4)!**

Watch these lessons (and make yourself a website) before continuing. It should not take you longer than an hour or two to get your website up. In addition to that, the WordPress platform is very intuitive, so you'll learn how to use it quickly and easily with trial and error.

Note: In these video lessons you will learn how to install free themes for your blog(s) or website(s). However, if you are trying to create a *professional* looking blog or website that attracts a vast and loyal readership (which you should be!), I would recommend looking into using premium themes designed by professional web designers (all my major websites use premium themes). They aren't expensive, are highly customizable in ways that free themes usually aren't, and will greatly increase the credibility of your blog or website.

The best resources for affordable premium WordPress themes can be found on the following page under "Premium Themes":

http://makemoneyfromhomelionsclub.com/resources

Conclusion

There is a lot more to this business than you probably thought, right? Don't be overwhelmed or feel discouraged by all the information! If you take the time to do the proper research, follow your own purchasing rules, list the tickets properly, and keep proper records, you can do extremely well in this business. After a while, you will realize that these little extras that you do (research, tracking, proper listings, etc.) will make you much more successful in this business. Once this all becomes second nature, you will realize this is one of the easiest businesses in the world to make really good money in. Good luck!

This ebook was brought to you by
http://makemoneyfromhomelionsclub.com.

If you are interested in entrepreneurship, making passive income online, and other ways to make money outside of a standard job, be sure to visit http://makemoneyfromhomelionsclub.com!

In the first video lesson you are taught the entire process of how http://mikeomarphotography.com was made from beginning to end, without the need of any coding knowledge, in under one hour!

With the lessons taught there, you will be able to make yourself a professional website with any kind of look that you want.

There are also lessons on Search Engine Optimization (SEO), social media promotion, making mailing lists, selling ebooks and other digital products, developing passive income online, and more. There are also lessons on how to make money with Google, Amazon, and ClickBank (all passive!).

My books:

HOW TO MAKE A WEBSITE OR BLOG: with WordPress WITHOUT Coding, on your own domain, all in under 2 hours.
http://makemoneyfromhomelionsclub.com/ebook1

HOW TO MAKE MONEY ONLINE: Learn how to make money from home with my step-by-step plan to build a $5000 per month passive income website portfolio (based on building 10 websites that make at least $500 per month each).
http://makemoneyfromhomelionsclub.com/ebook

HOW TO START A BLOG THAT PEOPLE WILL READ: How to create a website, write about a topic you love, develop a loyal readership, and make six figures doing it.
http://makemoneyfromhomelionsclub.com/ebookblog

CPSIA information can be obtained at www.ICGtesting.com
Printed in the USA
BVOW06s0231161015

422800BV00010B/60/P